Never Sew on a Rainy Day

To Joan
from Herb
Best wishes
Shirley Byers Lalonde

Weather Signs
Rhymes and Reasons

SHIRLEY BYERS LALONDE

Illustrated by Suzanne Lalonde

Canadian Cataloguing in Publication Data
Lalonde, Shirley, 1950-
Never sell your hen on a rainy day

Includes index.
ISBN 0-920923-11-9

1. Weather--Folklore. 2. Weather forecasting. I. Title.
QC998.L35 1997   398.26 C97-910801-2

Revised edition published 1998 by
Sandhill Publishing
#99-1270 Ellis Street
Kelowna, British Columbia V1Y 1Z4

First edition published 1994 by
Duck Creek Publications, Kelvington, Saskatchewan

Distributed by
Sandhill Book Marketing Ltd.
#99-1270 Ellis Street
Kelowna, British Columbia, Canada V1Y 1Z4

For orders, enquiries or author interviews
Phone: 250-763-1406 Fax: 250-763-4051
Email: Sandhill@wkpowerlink.com

Cover design by Jack Thompson
Illustrated by Suzanne Lalonde
Edited by Nancy Wise

Printed and bound in Canada

FOREWORD

I grew up hearing weather proverbs from my father. I took them for granted. After he was gone, I realized that there was so much I didn't know and wanted to know. *Why* were cows restless before a storm? *Why* did a mackerel sky indicate bad weather and a red sky at night good weather? *Why* could we hear our neighbour half a mile away so clearly just before a rain?

So began a study that has resulted in the creation of several articles and the book you are now holding. There are hundreds and hundreds of weather proverbs and some go back to at least the time of Christ. Since the beginning of time people have striven to understand and to predict the weather. It is the one thing that influences everything from how we feel physically to our country's economy.

Weather decides if the fisherman on the Atlantic coast will put out to sea. Even if all other factors, economic and otherwise are perfect, the weather can still devastate a prairie crop. It is weather that determines if the grasshoppers will be plentiful or few. Enough rain at the right time can rot the insect eggs. In the spring of 1997, the weather caused huge areas of Manitoba to be flooded, millions of dollars in damages to be incurred and even lives lost. As I write this, friends in Grand Forks, British Columbia are watching the Kettle River lapping at the out buildings at the back of their property. There is talk of a crest which could push the surging waters the few remaining feet to their house.

Small wonder our ancestors were weather watchers. Their livelihood, their well being, their very existence was dependent on the climate and its various moods and manifestations.

As our ancestors watched the weather, they began to notice certain patterns that seem to occur in nature. Sounds travelled further before a rain. Evening dew on the grass was a harbinger of a clear day on the morrow, a west wind seemed to bring good weather, dandelions closed their petals before a rain, animals became more active—these were just a few.

These correlations were proved correct time and time again. Weather proverbs were created. Sometimes they were written down but because very few people could read, the proverbs survived mostly by being repeated aloud. The rhyme form in which many were composed made them easier to remember. That is where weather proverbs have come from. Why they have survived is another story.

Though most of us will acknowledge that some of the old proverbs are pure superstition, it is also true that as many are trustworthy because they are based on scientific realities. Particularly in short term weather forecasting they are fairly reliable. You'll have the best percentage of wins in the weather forecasting world if you watch for a pattern. If the leaves are turning upside down, the cow is trying to scratch her ear, the dog is eating grass and the wind is blowing from the southeast, it is more likely that it will indeed rain than if just one of those things is taking place.

After I had written and self published the first edition of this book in 1994, I received countless letters and calls from people all across Canada. They wanted the book, which was very nice.

But most of them also wanted to chat. They wanted to thank me for writing the book. I remember one conversation in particular.

This fellow was from BC. He had obtained a copy of *Never Sell Your Hen on a Rainy Day* and was thoroughly delighted with it. He compared it to the Christmas cake he had made from his grandmother's recipe and shared with the rest of the staff at the school where he taught.

Home-made Christmas cakes, old recipes handed down, weather folklore—they all represent the past and as we feast on them we honour the past, we validate the wisdom of those who came before us and we enrich our spirits.

Shirley Byers Lalonde
Kelvington, Saskatchewan

Contents

In memory of my parents,
Jack and Doris Byers.

When the
Goose and the Gander
Begin to Meander

❧ CHAPTER 1

When the Goose and the Gander
Begin to Meander

A pressure system is a whirling air mass that moves across the earth, usually from west to east and rather like a spinning top moving across a surface. High pressure systems generally bring clear, sunny skies while low pressure systems are associated with clouds and precipitation.

A long, long time ago before radio, television and the six o'clock weather report, people lived close to nature. Many of them made their livings by working outdoors. Unaware of the concepts of pressure systems, they began to notice that when a certain thing happened in nature, usually a certain other thing happened in the weather. Over time these "forecasts" were made into sayings, often in the form of rhymes.

Because most people lived in rural areas, many of the rhymes had to do with animal behaviour. Animals still do a pretty good job of short term weather forecasting. Certain changes in the atmosphere affect them in ways that are readily apparent:

> *The goose and the gander*
> *Begin to meander.*

The matter is plain:
They are dancing for rain.

When the peacock loudly bawls
Soon you'll have both rain and squalls.

If crows make much noise
and fly round and round:
A sign of rain.

These pithy proverbs are based on the fact that birds have extremely sensitive hearing and can actually *hear* an approaching thunderstorm when it is still many miles away. Also their hollow feathers enable them to *feel* as well as hear low frequency sound waves.

Wild geese, wild geese
Going out to sea.
All fine weather it will be.

Wild geese wait on the Atlantic sea coast for the best flying weather and nobody goes anywhere until they get it. The geese seem to know when a storm is coming. How do they know? Probably those hollow-hearing feathers.

The *height* at which birds fly can tell you something about the sort of weather to expect:

Geese high
Fair sky.

Are you beginning to think that maybe geese aren't all that silly? Actually, they are some sharp birds. Now, they may not know that when barometric pressure is high, weather is usually good or that when it is low, weather is usually bad.

But geese do know enough to choose an altitude where the air is fairly dense, because dense or "thick" air provides more lift under their wings, making flying easier. On fair, high pressure days, this optimum level can be thousands of feet up. Conversely when a low pressure mass moves in, the "thickest" air and the best fly space is closer to the ground.

Birds flying low,
Expect rain and a blow.

Gulls, swallows and other birds will also be seen flying lower to the ground if rain is imminent. The smaller birds are similarly affected by the air density but they have another reason for lowering their altitude—*dinner.*

The insects which birds eat are greatly affected by the increased levels of *relative humidity* that occur prior to a rain. Moisture condenses on their bodies and makes flying difficult for mosquitoes, flies and other tiny, winged creatures. So insects fly lower where they are able to obtain some relief from that draggy feeling—which may be of little comfort when they end up in some bird's beak.

A domesticated bird, the rooster, can tell us if it's going to rain.

When the rooster crows
On going to bed,
You may rise with
A watery head.

Crowing is a territorial thing. Roosters do it to let other roosters know, "This is *my* yard. *My* chicken house. It's all *mine*!" The crowing is usually done in the morning as a bit of a tone-setter for the day and a reminder to any upstart who may be contemplating a "coup" in the coop.

Normally, roosters don't crow in the evening. But when they do, it could be a sign of increased irritability due to falling *barometric pressure*. The lowered atmospheric pressure that presages a storm causes all sorts of difficulties for Mr. Rooster. His body, like our bodies, must maintain an equilibrium with the air pressure around it.

In order to do that, when the air pressure falls, the rooster's body must give up dissolved gases or it would tend to expand and expand and expand and...*pouf!* Smithereens of rooster. But don't worry, that doesn't happen.

Body fluids gradually release these gases. As they do, the gases collect as small bubbles in body tissues. These bubbles affect nerve impulses and tend to make Mr. Rooster a tad peevish.

Animals are similarly affected:

When a horse is restless
And paws with its hoof,
You'll soon hear the patter
Of rain on your roof.

When a cow tries to scratch its ear
It means a shower is very near.
When it thumps its ribs with its tail:
Look out for thunder, lightning and hail.

Before a rain sheep are frisky
And box each other.

When the ass begins to bray
Surely rain will come that day.

Other unusual behaviour can be observed in household pets. One of the most common:

Cats and dogs eat grass before a rain.

Cats and dogs will eat grass before a rain because their stomachs feel upset. Their queasiness, like the rooster's irritability, is probably due to the falling barometric pressure. Often body itching accompanies this unwell feeling and animals will be seen scratching themselves more frequently than normal.

Horses rolling over in the pasture, a sign of rain.

Dogs rolling on their backs, expect rain.

When you see a pig scratch itself on a post,
it will rain soon.

If fowls roll in the sand,
Foul weather is at hand.

If you're an angler and like to fish, you may have noticed that fish bite better just before a rain:

Trout jump high
When a rain is nigh.

Fish bite better because they are closer to the surface just before a rain. But *why* are they closer to the surface? Again, it's because of that low pressure system that generally accompanies a storm. In good weather and bad, there is decaying plant matter on the bottom of lakes and rivers. This provides a home for nymphs or baby insects. It also produces a gas that clings to the decaying matter in the form of small bubbles.

During fair, high pressure weather, the matter and the gas pretty well stay on the bottom. But when barometric pressure begins to fall, exerting less outside pressure on the bubbles, they expand from the inside and begin to rise to the surface of the water, taking some of the decaying matter with them. Minnows start to feed on this rising matter. Larger fish swim up to feed on the minnows and in their enthusiasm, may chomp onto any fish hook that happens along.

Animals have a much keener sense of smell than people. Relative humidity is usually high just before a rain. This means the air is moist, and when it is, air moisture will attach to aromatic molecules. The moist aromatic molecules then bind more easily to the moist surfaces inside the nose where the sense of smell is located. Hence:

If dogs and horses sniff the air,
A summer shower will soon be there.

Dogs hunt better before a rain.

If cows and sheep sniff the air,
A sign of rain.

Some people claim they can "smell a rain coming" and they probably can. The same principles apply to human noses. I'll tell you more about this in chapter two.

If cats lick themselves, fair weather.

In fair weather when relative humidity is low, the air is dry and electrostatic charges can build up on a cat's fur. To make a long story short—Kitty becomes positively charged. That's why some cats don't like to be petted during cold, dry winter weather. Enough electricity builds up to cause little sparks. *Meeee-ow!*

But when a cat licks herself, the moisture makes her fur a better conductor and the charge can then "leak" off, making her much more comfortable.

Insects can also help us predict the weather. Spiders, ants and bees behave differently when a rain is coming and crickets can even tell us the temperature!

Strange as it may seem, this is true. Crickets are cold-blooded little creatures. Their body temperature is always the same as the air around them. And their level of activity is closely related to the temperature. (Hmm, sounds like people, doesn't it?) Crickets "chirp" by rubbing their wings together. The higher the temperature, the faster they rub and the more chirps they produce.

If you count the number of chirps in eight seconds and add four to that number, you will have the temperature in degrees Celsius. For Fahrenheit, count the chirps in fourteen seconds and add forty. Try it!

If spiders are busy with home maintenance chores
We soon can expect the rain to pour.

Before a rain, spiders can be seen scurrying around, catching up on home repairs. Picture in your mind, Sally and Stan Spider:

Sally (all eight hands on her hips): "It's going to rain, Stan. Don't you think you'd better fix up this web before we all get washed out to sea?"

Stan: "Yeah, yeah! I do all the upkeep on this place and what do I get?"

Sally: "You get to *live*, Stanley. Consider yourself fortunate to be married to a *progressive* spider. I could have eaten you long ago but I decided to break with tradition."

Stan (nervously): "Heh! Heh! Don't you know when I'm teasing you, Sweetie-spi? I'll get at those repairs right away, and I'll also build that deck you've been wanting and the fly-catcher off the kids' room, and the back entrance swing rope and it'll all be done before it rains. *I promise!*"

Well, maybe that's not quite the way it happens. Okay, Sally and Stan don't really *know* it's going to rain. They just know the web is falling apart and they'd better get it fixed before the next fly happens along.

During periods of high humidity before a rain, spider webs will absorb moisture. They become thick and tight and threads will break. Ropes made from plant fibre are also affected by increased relative humidity in much the same way as Sally and Stan's web. More about this later...

Step on a spider and it will rain.

If you're thinking this well known saying is just pure superstition, you're right. Stepping on a spider will *not* make it rain. If it could, can you imagine all the spider stomping that would go on in a prairie drought?

However, since spiders are more active before a rain (like our friend Stan), it would follow that we are more apt to see them at those times. And also more likely to step on them.

Expect stormy weather when ants
Travel in a straight line.
When they scatter all over
The weather is fine.

When an ant finds food, she begins to release a substance called *pheromone.* She hurries back to the ant hill to tell the other ants. *"Hey everybody! I found this fantastic picnic. C'mon! Follow the pheromone!"* And away they all go.

The pheromone is like a little bread crumb trail, leading everyone to the food source. But those insects have to hurry because the pheromone tends to drift. As you can imagine, this is very confusing, and accounts for much of the seemingly senseless dashing hither and yon that ants sometimes do.

On the other hand, if the *humidity is high* as it usually is before a rain, water in the air will attach to the pheromone molecules making them more stable and the scent trail much easier to follow. And the ants will travel in a straight line.

If bees to distance wing their flight
Days are warm and skies are bright.
When their flight ends close to home
Stormy weather's sure to come.

Bees will not swarm before a rain.

The reason why bees never get caught in the rain is quite simple. They will stay home or fly very short distances before a rain because they just can't go any further. Their navigation systems are shut down. You might say they are "fogged in".

Bees navigate with respect to polarized light from the sky. In clear weather, this is relatively simple—for a bee. However, before a rain, high cirrus clouds loaded with ice crystals scatter the sun's rays and destroy the polarization. Bees can't figure out where they're going, so they stay home.

A fogged in bee is a frustrated bee. Those little insects really live to get out and gather nectar. If bees are forced to stay indoors and do housework, they can get very cranky. So beware the stinging bee on cloudy days.

The Daisy Shuts Its Eye
Before a Rain

❧ CHAPTER 2

The Daisy Shuts Its Eye
Before a Rain

Plants can help us forecast the weather. These four old adages share a common principle:

> *The daisy shuts its eye before a rain.*

> *Now, look! Our weather glass is spread:*
> *The pimpernel whose flower*
> *Closes its leaves of spotted red*
> *Against a rainy hour.*

> *Dandelion blossoms close before a rain.*

> *If the chickweed should shut up,*
> *Then the traveller is to put on his greatcoat.*

Harbingers of summer rains, these plants close their petals when the relative humidity of the air near the ground reaches about eighty per cent. Rain frequently does fall when the relative humidity increases to this extent.

Besides providing a convenient weather predictor for us, this reaction also has benefits for the plant. The dandelion, for example, even while it is beautifying your lawn, is busy producing seeds and attaching fine, silky fibres to them. These fibres will become the little parachutes which will carry the dandelion's seeds far and wide. If those parachutes-in-the- making were to become wet, they wouldn't be able to travel. The flower closes to prevent this from happening.

While some plants close their petals or their "eye" when the humidity rises and the probability of rain increases, at least one plant has been designed to do the opposite. The leaves of the Pitcher Plant are jug–shaped with a hood surrounded by downward pointing bristles. These bristles act to direct any water into the cup of the leaf. The Pitcher Plant opens wider before a rain.

The increased relative humidity that occurs before a rain also has an effect on the scents of flowers.

> *The lovely rose and all aromatic flowers*
> *Smell extra sweet just before a shower.* *

The water molecules in the air adhere to the flower's aromatic molecules, giving them a moist coating which allows them in turn, to attach more easily to moist surfaces inside our noses. Flowers smell better before a rain because more of the scent, which is normally lost, reaches our noses.

The same, unfortunately, is true of less agreeable odours. ʼaying plant matter in a long-ago ditch or pond inspired 'thy little rhyme:

> *When ditches and ponds offend the nose*
> *Look for rain and stormy blows.*

Increased relative humidity has effects on other plants:

When moss is soft and moist,
Expect rain.

When corn fodder stands all dry and crisp,
Go on your outing, there's no great risk.

Corn fodder, I'm assuming, relates to corn stalks and ears that have been harvested to feed to cattle and pigs. Yet, the reference to it standing would seem to imply that it is still in the field. In any case, increased moisture in the air makes for damp corn fodder, a sign of rain, whereas dry corn fodder is obviously a sign of good weather.

Although not as common as they once were, there are still many ropes made from plant fibres. These natural fibres are hollow on the inside. As soon as the relative humidity starts to climb, water molecules from the air enter these tiny, fibre-encased tubes and condenses into liquid water, causing the rope to swell and contract along its length. As the relative humidity rises so does the likelihood of rain. Ropes shorten and knots get tighter before a rain.

While humidity affects some plants, others are temperature sensitive:

Open crocus,
Warm weather.
Closed crocus,
Cold weather.

Scientists have checked this idea out and have found that it is possible to tell the air temperature to the closest one-half degree by noting how far the crocus has opened. Tulips are similarly affected. They open their petals when the temperature rises, but close them when it falls.

Miss Tulip's shy in weather cold,
In warmer times, her face is bold. *

Grass is one of the most common plant forms. We grow it, mow it, weed it and some of us even feed it. Because it's such a great dew-catcher we can also use grass as a weather forecaster.

Dew forms on evenings when the grass and other objects cool more quickly that the air around them. Moisture in the air condenses into the moist covering we call dew. A clear, calm night usually produces dew.

But if the night sky is cloudy, the clouds act like warm, fuzzy blankets and the grass will not cool quickly enough for dew to form. Dew will generally not form if the night is windy or muggy since these conditions tend to prevent the ground from cooling more quickly than the surrounding air.

When the dew is on the grass
Rain will never come to pass.

When the grass is dry at morning light,
Look for rain before the night!

The same conditions that precede a rain, such as mugginess, clouds and wind, also make for a dewless night. The conditions that produce dew tend to accompany good weather, so both of these sayings are logical and very often correct.

These weather rhymes work well in relation to Poplar, Maple and Cottonwood trees:

> *When the leaves show their undersides*
> *Be very certain that rain betides.*

> *Trees are light green*
> *When the weather is fair;*
> *They turn quite dark*
> *When a storm is in the air.*

Damp air caused by increased humidity softens leaf stalks, allowing the leaves to be more easily lifted by breezes and by rising currents of heated air that occur before a local shower or thunderstorm.

Mushrooms and toadstools are fungi and not true plants, but they are canny, wee weather watchers.

> *If a toadstool greets you 'ere morning's flight*
> *Look for rain before the night.* *

> *Mushrooms popping up in the grass,*
> *Rain will surely come to pass.* *

Mushrooms and toadstools need a fairly moist environment and thrive in the relative humidity that precedes a summer rain. If you find them appearing all over your yard, don't be surprised if the rains follow soon.

Author's note:
You'll notice that some verses are marked with an asterisk. In instances where no verse could be found, I created these to help illustrate some common and not-so-common weather observations and principles. All others are proverbs and rhymes discovered in my research.

Red Sky at Night
Sailors Delight

❧ CHAPTER 3

Red Sky at Night, Sailors Delight

To our ancestors, the sky was a huge weather map. They didn't have televisions, radios and newspapers but they knew how to read the sky. One of the oldest weather rhymes tells us that a red sky can forecast fair or foul weather:

Red sky at night,
Sailors delight!
Red sky in the morning—
Sailors take warning!

In Canada, as in many parts of the world, weather moves from *west to east.* In other words, if it is raining in Manitoba tonight, it may very well be raining in Ontario tomorrow. If the *evening* sky is red as the sun sets in the west, it is likely caused by the reflection of the sun's rays on minute particles suspended in the air. It would follow that there are no clouds between the sun and us and therefore no rain coming from the west.

On the other hand, a red sky in the *morning* is most

likely to occur when drier, clearer air is moving to the east and an advancing low pressure system is bringing rain in from the west.

A similar rhyme is closely related. In this one, the author is most concerned about the shepherd, and rightly so. In the days when the rhyme was created, a shepherd and his sheep were pretty much at the mercy of the elements. I'm not sure if we have any shepherds in Canada and if we do, they probably come equipped with rainsuits and all-terrain vehicles. Still, they would do well to remember:

> *A rainbow in the morning*
> *Is the shepherd's warning.*
> *A rainbow at night*
> *Is the shepherd's delight!*

If you're a clever shepherd, you've probably already deduced that this rhyme is also based on the west to east movement of our weather systems.

Since a rainbow can be seen only when facing the rain shower, with the sun at your back, a morning rainbow will be in the west and a sign of rain moving *towards* you from that direction. Conversely, a rainbow in the evening is seen in the east. This indicates that the rain has *passed* and is moving *away* to the east. So look out, all you shepherds in the east!

Clouds change as the moisture content and temperature patterns alter in the air. Changes in the weather are foreshadowed in the *shape, positioning, movement* and *height* of the clouds.

Mackerel sky, mackerel sky;
Never long wet, never long dry.

A mackerel sky is clouded by rounded, isolated, cirrocumulus clouds that look like mackerel scales or herring bones. They are made up of ice crystals and may travel at speeds up to 160 kilometres an hour, six to eleven kilometres above the earth. A mackerel sky often forms in thundery weather which is neither wet nor dry for very long. A variation of the proverb is:

Mackerel sky, twenty-four hours dry.

Because of the conditions that go along with a mackerel sky, we often have rain the day after its appearance.

Other cloud shapes are also early forerunners of bad weather:

Hens' scarts and mares' tails
Make lofty ships carry low sails.

Hens'scarts, or scratchings, and mares' tails are high-in the-sky wisps of ice-laden cirrus clouds. These kinds of clouds are the first outriders of an approaching low pressure system bringing high winds and blustery weather.

The *positioning* of clouds can also be used to forecast the weather. It is an old saying that

The weather will be clear when
there is enough blue in the northwest
to make a leprechaun's jacket.

Low pressure systems bringing snow or rain contain many layers of cloud. A hole in the lower layers usually exposes only higher layers. If you see a patch of blue sky among the clouds, particularly in the northwest, it means that the storm centre has passed and is moving toward the east.

Clouds generally move together and in the same direction. Clouds moving in *different directions at different levels* are a sign of unsettled weather.

> *When crazy clouds go opposite ways*
> *Weather's uncertain in coming days.* *

High cirrus clouds and falling barometric pressure go along with the shifty clouds. While these cloud movements often foretell the onset of a low pressure system, it is usually a fairly fast moving system and the weather that goes with it is "iffy" at best.

Slow moving storm clouds that seem to have been hanging over our shoulders for days are usually the offspring of a very slow-moving storm that will eventually rain on us for a day or maybe two or three.

> *Rain long foretold, long last;*
> *Short notice, soon past.*

On the other hand, clouds which seem to come rapidly out of nowhere are more likely to be part of a flashy squall that will soon blow over.

> *When clouds appear*
> *like rocks and towers,*
> *The Earth's refreshed*
> *with frequent showers.*

Towering clouds go way, *way* up. These clouds are loaded with moisture and rising. They are rising because the zillions of tiny water droplets of which they are made, are condensing. As they condense, they give off heat, rendering the cloud warmer than the surrounding air. And warm air always rises. As the top of the cloud builds higher, more and more of it condenses until raindrops form.

The night sky can give us some tips as to the upcoming weather. Check out those stars!

A twinkling north star
Will probably bring rain.

When on a bed of black, the stars do flicker,
Soon you'll be lookin' for your rain slicker. *

When the stars twinkle and some fade entirely to black, it is an indication of unstable air between us and the star. The greater the instability, the greater the likelihood for rain or snow.

On a spring or fall evening, the clearer and calmer the air, the greater the chance for frost. Clouds which diffuse the moon and starlight also act as an insulating blanket over the earth. So, when the stars and the moon are shining crystal clear, tuck a blanket around those tomatoes! You might also want to tuck a blanket around yourself because:

Clear moon,
Frost soon.

A ring around the moon is lovely to see. The ring is also a reliable weather sign:

If the moon shows a silver shield,
Be not afraid to reap your field;
But if she rises, haloed round,
Soon we'll tread on deluged ground.

Ring around the moon,
Rain is coming soon.

A halo or ring around the moon is caused by moonlight shining through ice-laden cirrus clouds. Cirrus clouds are the early harbingers of an approaching low pressure system, often appearing at least 1500 km ahead of the centre of the low.

Rays of moonlight are bent or refracted as they pass through the ice crystals that make up these clouds, and the result is a haloed moon. When the clouds are thin, the halo is dim. As the storm approaches, the clouds contain more ice crystals and the halo becomes brighter. The brighter the halo, the nearer the rain or snow.

The bigger and brighter the ring,
The nearer the wet.

The probability of precipitation after the sighting of a halo is even greater in winter because winter storm systems are better developed, travel faster and live longer.

When the Forest Murmurs and the Mountain Roars

CHAPTER 4

When the Forest Murmurs and the Mountain Roars

My dad always said that it was going to rain when we could hear the neighbour kids on the next farm as well as if they were in our yard. And it always did.

Sounds travelling far and wide
A rainy day will betide.

Sounds *do* travel better just before a rain. There are two reasons why. On a clear day, the surfaces of the earth are heated unevenly. For example, a beach will be hotter than the lake and a summerfallow field will be hotter than a grassy pasture.

This uneven heating produces up-and-down currents in the air. These currents tend to scatter sound waves and some of them are lost.

However, when the sky is *overcast* and the air is *humid*, clouds block the amount of solar radiation reaching the earth. The air at ground level cools and evens out. The up-and-down currents are neutralized. So, just before a rain-storm, the lower air is of an even temperature and free of sound-juggling currents. Sounds will travel further.

The second reason has to do with *inversions*. Normally, the atmosphere gets colder the higher up you go. But when an inversion occurs, usually before a rain, temperatures actually *increase* with height.

Sound travels both horizontally and vertically. Sound travels faster in warm air. Upward moving sound waves are usually slowed down and lost in the cold upper air. But the warm upper air of an inversion catches sounds and allows them to zip along, reaching the listener at the same time as the slightly slower moving horizontal waves. Thus, during an inversion a child's vigorous shout would be twice as loud and might be heard almost a kilometre away. These rhymes are based on the same principles:

> *When the forest murmurs and the mountain roars,*
> *Then close your windows and shut your doors.*

> *When the peacock loudly bawls,*
> *Soon we'll have both rain and squalls.*

According to the following rhyme, an absence of squalls, gales and winds of all kinds means fair weather:

> *No weather is ill*
> *If the wind is still.*

Now, if you've ever experienced a prairie winter, you might take exception to this and who could blame you? Very cold, bone-chilling, mind-numbing weather can and does occur when the wind is perfectly still.

In winter, clouds act as huge blankets insulating the earth somewhat from the cold temperatures at higher altitudes. But when a high pressure system clears away those clouds, the temperature drops, wind or no wind.

In summer, however, this rhyme is quite logical and very often correct. A great deal of wind is caused by heat energy released by clouds. And if there are no clouds, then rain, hail or snow is unlikely.

Listening to the wind can give us an indication of what kind of weather we might expect.

> *When telephone lines whistle and hum*
> *They tell of a storm, soon to come.*

Such winds are called aeolian winds, named after Aeolus, Greek god of the winds. While most telephone lines are underground these days and most weather proverbs were written long before the advent of telephones, this saying is also true of any object that interrupts the wind's path and produces a whistling sound. This proverb probably also works because of the tendency of sound to travel better before a storm. In cold weather, telephone lines would tighten, producing a louder noise and cold weather is often followed by a storm.

Wind direction is another good indicator of what kind of weather to expect.

> *Wind from the south*
> *Has rain in its mouth.*

A wind from the south often heralds an approaching low pressure system. As it blows clouds nearer, humidity increases and so does the chance of rain.

A pressure system, as I've mentioned before, is a whirling mass that moves across the earth, usually from west to east, rather like a spinning top. In a high pressure system, the air as wind moves *clockwise* around the centre of the high. Wind moves *counter-clockwise* in a low pressure system. South, southeast and easterly winds generally accompany a low pressure system.

> *When the wind is in the east*
> *Tis good for neither man nor beast.*

The flow of air in a counter-clockwise movement around the centre of a low pressure system causes an easterly wind. As pressure falls, all types of precipitation can occur.

When I was growing up, our farm was a few miles from the Pasquia Hills which normally were coloured a soft blue-grey. When the hills were a darker blue and seemed to be closer, someone might remark that rain was coming. And they were usually right.

> *When hills put on a coat of deepest blue*
> *And move across the fields to you*
> *Expect rain.* *

This phenomenon occurs when a *southeast wind* brings in moisture. The warm air at ground level rises, forming a mirage. The hills appear to be closer, and the moist air often produces rain.

If rain isn't what you want, look for a north wind:

> *A northern air*
> *Brings fair weather.*

The wind usually shifts to the north or northwest when a *high pressure system* is coming towards us. North, northwest and westerly winds usually go with a high pressure system. During high pressure periods, people generally feel better. This rhyme offers a bit of good advice:

> *Do business best*
> *When the wind is in the west.*

High pressure in the summer means good weather while a low is often accompanied by lowered temperatures, clouds and precipitation. In winter, however, that cloud-bearing low pressure system, while still bringing precipitation, will actually allow the temperature to rise because the clouds insulate the earth from the cold air in the upper atmosphere. The clear skies of a winter high pressure system will make for lower temperatures.

> *The winds of daytime wrestle and fight,*
> *Longer and stronger than those of the night.*

> *The west wind is a gentleman and goes to bed.*

All winds tend to decrease at night, at least at ground level. As the sun goes down, the ground cools and reaches a temperature very close to that of the upper air. Since wind is air movement caused by the mixing of air at different temperatures, we often see a definite calming of winds as the night deepens.

Wind direction can be a helpful tool in do-it-yourself weather forecasting even when the wind can't decide *which* way to blow:

When the wind's undecided which way to blow
And clouds roll and pitch, expect rain or snow. *

The vacillation of the wind is a result of unstable air, a situation in which clouds form and precipitation in the form of a rain or snow storm is likely.

Keep an eye on the clouds. They'll tell you which way the wind is blowing way up there. Sometimes, the wind blows in *different directions* at *different levels* of the atmosphere. When you first see clouds moving in a direction opposite to that of the wind on the ground, you may think your eyes are playing tricks on you. What you are actually seeing is something called *wind shear*.

When clouds move against the wind,
It is called a wind shear.
Could be that cold weather
Soon will be here. *

Wind shear is strong along a cold front and when we see this happening we can be fairly sure cold weather is on its way.

When the changes in the wind's direction are a little more subtle, the wind is said to be *veering* or *backing* with altitude. When wind direction swings from *east to south* or clockwise as it moves upward, the wind is said to be *veering* with altitude. If the wind changes from *east to north*, it is turning counter-clockwise and is said to be *backing* with altitude.

If a wind is veering, then warmer air is moving in. On the other hand, if the wind is backing with altitude, it means that colder air is on its way.

When You Look
in the Mirror and
It's a Bad Hair Day

❦ CHAPTER 5

When You Look in the Mirror and It's a Bad Hair Day

You don't have to be a country dweller to be your own weather forecaster. Certain changes in the atmosphere can be observed in the comfort of your own home, no matter where you live.

Pour yourself a cup of coffee and observe. When bubbles rise on the surface of coffee and hold together, it's a sign of good weather. If the bubbles break up, poor weather is coming.

> *Bubbles rising in your coffee cup*
> *In fair weather you will sup.*
> *But if they break and burst apart*
> *Rainy weather soon will start.* *

The bubbles on the surface of your coffee are full of trapped air. If the barometric pressure or air pressure around them is high, they will pretty much remain as they are. If the barometric pressure has dropped, as it will before a rain, the pressure *inside* the bubbles will be greater that the pressure *around* them and they will burst.

Now that you have that cup of coffee, come have a seat by the fire, because

When down the chimney falls the soot
Mud will soon be under foot. *

Chimney soot is mostly composed of carbon particles. These particles are very porous and they absorb gases during periods of high barometric pressure. When the barometric pressure begins to fall, trapped gas is released. As it is released, it takes some of the soot with it—down your chimney.

If you use candles, you may have noticed that they burn dimmer before a rain.

Candlelight, candlelight;
Before a shower, not as bright. *

The high humidity that occurs before a rain can cause your candles to burn less brightly. The wick, particularly if not treated with wax, will absorb moisture from the air. Water vapour in the air will also decrease the amount of available oxygen.

At least one salt manufacturer has added an anti-stick ingredient to its product but this little proverb also works well with sugar.

If salt is sticky,
And gains in weight,
It will rain
Before too late.

Salt and sugar take and retain moisture from the air. The more moist the air, the more readily the grains will stick. Lumpy salt and sugar can be a sign of a rain storm because of the moist air that can precede it.

I think the writer of the next proverb was probably referring to the old-fashioned oiled wood floors that are seldom seen nowadays. If you have such a floor, you might want to check this one out. Carefully.

> *Oily floors quite slippery get,*
> *Before the rain makes everything wet.*

Ever notice how windows and doors seem to stick just before a rain?

> *When doors and windows start to stick,*
> *Rain will soon our shingles lick.* *

A wooden door or window frame has itty-bitty veins that once, when the door was in the tree stage, carried nutrients up and down. During periods of high relative humidity, water condenses in these veins and makes the wood swell. The door or window is now larger and no longer fits as well in its frame. Likewise:

> *Catchy drawer and sticky door,*
> *Coming rain will pour and pour.* *

When relative humidity is high, humans are also affected. Just looking in the mirror can give you big clues about the upcoming weather. If you can't do a thing with your hair, maybe it's because of the weather:

> *When you look in the mirror*
> *And it's a bad hair day,*
> *Sign of rain-clouds*
> *Headed your way.* *

Stroll over to your window and check out any smoke coming from your neighbour's chimney. If smoke falls to the ground, it is likely to rain.

Smoke is heavy, falling down
Rain will soon wash the ground. *

Smoke is made up of bezillions of tiny particles. So tiny, that often there are many particles too small for us to see. In periods of high relative humidity or just before a rain, the smoke particles collect water molecules from the air, become heavier and fall to the ground.

Watching smoke is also an easy way to tell which way the wind is blowing. And of course, wind direction will tell you something about upcoming attractions, weather-wise:

When smoke goes west,
Good weather is past;
When smoke goes east,
Good weather comes niest [next].

Smoke going *west* indicates an *easterly* wind. Smoke going *east*, a *westerly* wind. An approaching low pressure system, bringing cloudy skies, is usually accompanied by winds from the south, east or southeast. On the other hand, high pressure systems with clear skies are usually accompanied by winds from the north, west, or northwest.

A previous chapter looked at how animals are affected by the barometric pressure changes that precede a change in the weather. Humans are similarly affected:

Men work better, eat more and sleep
sounder when barometric pressure is high.

God designed us in such a way that our bodies are able to adjust to the changes of barometric pressure in the air which surrounds us. As the barometric pressure changes, our body fluids absorb or give up gases. This equalizes our internal pressure and keeps us from exploding or collapsing.

When the barometric pressure is high during clear weather, our bodies absorb gases. When barometric pressure is low with cloudy, unsettled weather, our bodies give up some of these gases. It is in the giving up of gases that problems occur. And these problems are felt more acutely in injured tissue:

When your joints all start to ache,
Rainy weather is at stake.

If your corns all ache and itch,
The weather fair will make a switch.

So, with all the aches and pains and grumpy feelings that seem to accompany a low pressure system, is it any wonder that some long-ago sage penned this bit of weather wisdom?

Never sell your hen on a rainy day!

If Bears
Lay Up Food
in the Fall

❦ CHAPTER 6

If Bears Lay Up Food in the Fall

Though most meteorologists agree that *short term* weather signs and rhymes are quite reliable, most also agree that when it comes to *long term* forecasts, the credibility gap widens.

The thickness of the deer's fur, the size of the squirrel's winter store of nuts and the width of the woolly bear caterpillar's brown band have all been said to indicate the length and severity of the oncoming winter.

The woolly bear, by the way, is that furry little brown and black caterpillar who shows up in your backyard every autumn. It's a very cute little creature with three distinct bands of colour: black, brown in the middle and another black band. It is the *brown middle band* to watch. It is said that the greater its width, the milder the oncoming winter.

About forty years ago, some enterprising individuals decided to check out this caterpillar theory once and for all. They gathered woolly bears, measured brown bands and there was no doubt about it. Thin brown belly bands foretold a long, white winter. Those who took their caterpillars seriously stocked up on food, fuel and board games—only to experience one of the mildest winters in years.

Some animals have earned their own proverbs:

If bears lay up food in the fall,
Expect a cold winter.

When skunks are fat, the winter will be long.

The breastbone of the Thanksgiving turkey or goose was often employed in winter weather predicting. If half of the bone was brown and half was white, winter would be cold at first, but warm up in January or February. Another proverb held that if the breastbone of the Thanksgiving goose was red or had many spots, then a cold, stormy winter was in the offing. However, if only a few spots were visible, the winter would be mild.

Groundhog Day, on February 2, was originally celebrated as *Candlemas,* a feast day of the early church.

Candlemas day, Candlemas day
Half your wood and half your hay.

The hope was that on this day, winter would be at least half over. If you were fortunate, maybe more than half over.

Various other animals such as the badger, the hedgehog and the bear were drawn into the Candlemas lore.

At the day of Candlemas,
Cold in the air, and snow on the grass;
If the sun then entice the bear from his den,
He turns around thrice and goes back again.

This belief began in Europe hundreds of years ago. The groundhog only came into the picture when the legend made its way to North America with the early settlers.

I could never keep the precepts of Groundhog Day straight when I was a kid. It seemed to me that a sensible groundhog is more apt to stay above the ground if the sun *is* shining enough for him to see his shadow. But that's not the way the story goes.

If he *doesn't* see his shadow, then he *doesn't* go back to bed and we've seen the last of winter. Well, that's the theory. It isn't guaranteed one hundred per cent accurate, especially in parts of Canada where on February 2 we can count on *at least* six weeks more of winter, shadow or no shadow. But never mind, it's all in fun and a harmless bit of notoriety for an often overlooked rodent.

Plants have also been used as indicators in long term weather forecasting. When the Mountain Ash tree produces lots of berries, it is thought to be a prediction of a severe winter. Another old adage says that plenty of blossoms on the Walnut tree is a sign of a fruitful year.

At first glance, proverbs that predict the following season based on the condition of a tree, plant or vegetable may seem a little doubtful.

Onion skin very thin
Mild winter coming in;
Onion skin thick and tough,
Coming winter, cold and rough.

However, many of these sayings are based on a fairly widespread belief that nature always averages things out so that we can remain close to normal. Hence, a cold summer will be followed by a warm winter or a mild winter by an inclement spring.

A cold rainy summer might well produce a thin skinned,

mild mannered onion, whereas a hot, dry summer is more likely to bring forth a robust, tough skinned bulb. This rhyme is telling us that if the summer is cool, we can expect a warm winter. Conversely, if the summer is warm, we can expect a cold or "rough" winter. Right or wrong, this theory of balance accounts for a plethora of proverbs such as:

Who doffs his coat on a winter's day,
Will gladly put it on in May

A warm November is a sign of a cold winter.

If February gives much snow
A fine summer is doth show.

If March comes in like a lion, it goes out like a lamb.
If March comes in like a lamb, it goes out like a lion.

Wet May, dry July.

As high as the weeds grow,
So will the banks of snow.

If the spring be cold and wet
The autumn will be cold and dry.

"We'll pay for this!" the naysayers warned us in November and December of 1997 as *El Nino* brought shirt-sleeve weather to the Canadian prairies and elsewhere. As the old year slipped away, temperatures began falling and falling and falling. Those of us who had doffed our coats were indeed gladly putting them back on, along with sweaters, scarves and mittens.

Many, many rhymes were written in a well-meaning, if misguided, attempt to give honour to a saint, such as this ninth century Scottish proverb:

> *St. Swithin's Day if ye do rain,*
> *For forty days it will remain.*
> *St. Swithin's Day and ye be fair,*
> *For forty days 'twill rain nae mair.*

St. Swithin, a bishop of Winchester, was a humble and self-effacing man in life and, it seems, in death as well. He gave the order that when he died, he was to be buried "in a vile and unworthy place, under the drip of the eaves." In those days, this would have been a very radical request. Bishops and others of their ilk were traditionally entombed inside the walls of the cathedral. Swithin's wishes were carried out, but not, one infers, without much muttering and murmuring.

Finally, in 971, the monks of Winchester decided that enough was enough. The good Saint had made his point, but now it was time to bring him inside where he belonged. Plans were made for the move to take place with suitable pomp and fanfare on July 15 of that year.

But on the appointed day, a huge rain began to fall and continued for forty days. Swithin was allowed to remain in his original burial site and soon after, the rhyme appeared. And so, the unassuming Saint, who wanted no memorial, is remembered more than a thousand years later.

Other saints have been similarly immortalized. Each month of the year has at least one saint's day with its accompanying weather proverb:

January 25th: St. Paul's Day
> *If St. Paul's be fair and clear*
> *It doth foretell a happy year.*

> *But, if by chance it should rain*
> *It will make dear all kinds of grain.*

February 6: St. Dorothea's Day
> *St. Dorothea gives the most snow.*

March 17: St. Patrick's Day
> *The warm side of a stone turns up*
> *And the broadback goose begins to lay.*

April 5: St. Vincent's Day
> *If St. Vincent's be fair,*
> *there will be more water than wine.*

May 26: St. Phillip's Day
> *When it rains on St. Phillip's Day*
> *the poor will need no help from the rich.*

June 11: St. Barnabus' Day
> *On St. Barnabus' Day, the sun comes to stay.*

July 22: St. Mary Magdalene's Day
> *St. Mary washes her handkerchief.*

August 24: St. Bartholomew's Day
> *If this day is misty with frost in the morning,*
> *cold weather will come soon and bring a cold winter.*

September 29: Michaelmas Day
> *As many days old the moon on Michaelmas*
> *As many floods after.*

October 28: St. Jude's Day
> *On St. Jude's Day the oxen may play;*
> *November take flail, let more ships sail.*

November 11: St. Martin's Day
If the leaves do not fall before St. Martin's
Expect a hard winter.

December 26: St. Stephen's Day
St. Stephen's Day windy, bad for next year's grapes.

Other saints immortalized in verses are St. Peter, St. Mathias and St. Valentine to name a few. Sayings related to saints date from the Middle Ages and earlier. Today, a saints' day does not occur on its original date due to the institution of the Gregorian calendar in 1582.

Proverbs have been coined for other special days:

The twelve days of Christmas determine the weather of each
month of the year.

When the sun is shining on Shrove Tuesday,
it means well for the rye and peas.

A bad palm Sunday denotes a year of failing crops.

If it thunders on All Fools Day,
it will bring good crops of corn and hay.

Superstition has endowed not only saints' days and holidays with power over the weather. The days of the week, especially Friday and Sunday have been thought to possess a similar ability:

If the sun sets clear on Friday
It will blow before Sunday night.

If it storms on the first Sunday of the month,
It will storm every Sunday.

The last Sunday of the month
indicates the weather of the next month.

These beliefs may have evolved because, for most people then, Sunday was the one day off work and was often spent outdoors with more time to notice the weather.

It is true that many of the long term forecasting proverbs seem to be based on pure superstition. Some, like the following pair, simply contradict each other:

If the ash is out before the oak
You may expect a thorough soak;
If the oak is out before the ash,
You'll hardly get a single splash.

If the oak is out before the ash
'Twill be a summer of wet and splash;
But if the ash is before the oak,
'Twill be a summer of fire and smoke.

It could be argued that there is a scientific basis for some of the long term weather proverbs and we just haven't found it yet. After all, the short term sayings that have been proven to be true were pooh-poohed for years. And similar sayings did evolve in different countries, thousands of miles apart from each other when travel to and communication between them were non-existent. The British hedgehog that became the North American groundhog also had an Asian counterpart.

And so, perhaps, did the woolly bear caterpillar.

ACKNOWLEDGEMENTS

Several books were of invaluable help in researching the material for this book. I recommend them to anyone who would like to pursue the subject further.

Freier, George D. *Weather Proverbs*, Tucson:Fisher Books, 1989

Garriot, Edward B. *Weather Folklore and Local Weather Signs,* Detroit:Gale, 1971

Hornstein, Reuben A. *The Weather Book,* Toronto: McClelland and Stewart, 1980

Swainson, C. *A Handbook of Weather Folklore,* Detroit: Gale, 1974

I would also like to acknowledge the information and encouragement I received from Environment Canada. Particular thanks are due to Dave Zaluski, formerly of the Wynyard Weather Station and now in Regina, and Marv Lassi, at the Northeast Saskatchewan District Office in Yorkton.

If you'd like to share a weather proverb, rhyme or a weather story, we'd love to hear from you. Please contact us at:

Sandhill Publishing
#99-1270 Ellis Street
Kelowna, Britsh Columbia
Canada V1Y 1Z4

INDEX